Burn the Fairy Tales

by Adeline Whitmore

## burn the fairy tales

burn the tropes
kill off the defenseless
princess
and the rapey prince
let the woman
fend
for her damn self
and lets toss away
all this bullshit
and finally get rid
of these ancient ideas

let the woman
rise

<u>chapter one</u>
kill the prince

<u>chapter two</u>
give the princess a sword

<u>chapter three</u>
send her into battle

<u>chapter four</u>
watch her win

Chapter One
<u>Kill The Prince</u>

\#

## the prince

the prince
is not a hero
by virtue
of his gender
and blood line

he is a villain
wanting praise
for allowing women
the smallest gains
in life

## kill the prince

kill the prince

move his
man-spreading
"not-all-men"-ing
mansplaining
ass
out of the way

let the women
who work for the limelight
have it
for once

## whole

you
were whole
before him

you
are still whole
without him

do not
define yourself
by him

define yourself
by yourself

for you are as whole
as you've ever been
and even more so

## defined

your beauty
is not defined
by the views
of men

your beauty
is deep within
emanating
from a deep inner spring

reach into it
and draw strength
to be
who you truly are

woman

they don't understand
what its like
to be catcalled
on a day to day basis

they don't know the fear
of existing
in the same space
as men

they don't understand
the enormous strength
it takoo
to just exist as a woman
on a day to day basis

you are so much stronger
than they
will ever give you
credit for

you are
a woman

<u>you are</u>

you are strong
you are beautiful
you are amazing

you will meet
the challenges
in your life

you will rise
above the pain

you are
everything
you need to be
at this moment

## double standards

a woman is a slut
for sleeping with men
but a man is a hero
for sleeping with women

a woman is shrill
if she yells
and a man
is just passionate

a woman is a distraction
for having a bra strap
and boys will be boys
and their actions are excused

we must stand up
to these double standards
and demand
to be treated
like a goddamn
human being

<u>today</u>

love
every curve

cherish
every stretch mark

adore
every part of you

just love
yourself
a little extra
today

you deserve it

## dragon

you are not
the damsel
in distress

you are the dragon
bringing fear
to the hearts
of men

so breathe your fire
and unleash
your strength
on the world

they will never know
what hit them

## beautiful

everything about you
is so beautiful

don't let anyone
tell you differently

## depths

i'm not interested
in small talk

let me peak
into the depths
of your soul

let's throw away
the societal norms

and fall fiercely in love
with each other

do not cover up
any piece
of your true self

bitch

be proud
of being labeled
a bitch

it means
you stood up
for your right
to exist
as a woman

wear that word
as a badge of pride

and don't let anyone
tell you
differently

give

you have been broken
in ways
no one else
could ever understand

but that just means
you have so much more
to give
than anyone else

problem

the problem
was never with you
so stop looking back
and thinking
of what
you could've done
differently

nothing
could have changed
the fact
that he
wasn't mature enough
to handle
who you are

## life

save the worries
and cares
and indecision
for death

for death
will never tire
of these things

but life
is eaten up
by them

so go
and live your life
the way life
was meant
to be lived

## 12

don't let your loneliness
convince you
he's worth your time

he's not
so stay strong
and wait for someone
who's just as into you
at noon
as he is
at midnight

diamonds

women
are capable
of going through the fire
and melding themselves
into something beautiful

we
can make diamonds
from ashes

and theres nothing
more beautiful
than that

garbage

stop wasting your time
thinking about men
who only think about you
in disgusting ways

throw him out
with the rest
of the garbage

## if he really loved you

if he really loved you
he wouldn't have cheated

end of story.

## real men

real men
are not afraid
of a woman's
sexuality
strength
or power

stop caring
about the feelings
of boys

they don't
fucking matter

## don't

don't waste
attention
sunsets
kisses
or love

on men
who don't
deserve them

rise

you were broken
you were at rock bottom
you were
at the end
of your strength

but look up
for the sun is rising
and you
will rise
with it

<u>sex</u>

if he only
cares
about his orgasm
during sex

it's not really sex
its him using
your body
to masturbate

and you should never
let a man
like that
use you

## want

your gut
already knows
what you want

shush the mind
stop overthinking things
go out
into this vast world
and take
what you want

## sex pt 2

if a man
has sex
with a woman
who is

unconscious
drugged
drunk
or doesn't
actively consent

it's rape
end of story

## problem

those
who pretend to be
feminists
yet defend
their rapist friends

are not real feminists
they are
the problem

<u>chapter two</u>
give the princess a sword

#

## give the princess a sword

you don't need a man
to defend you

why shouldn't it be
a woman
under a suit of armor?

throw away your assumptions
and let
women
defend
themselves

## assumptions

people
automatically picture
men
when they think
of
doctors
lawyers
politicians
and strength

and that
needs to change

for women
can be all that
and more

## object

you are not
an object

your body is not
for the enjoyment
of men
to look at
and touch

you
are your own
and you
are beautiful

## GOP

the republican party
is anti women
anti choice
and pro evil

and any woman
who votes for them
is an uncle tom

feminist

do you believe
that men and women
should be treated
equally?

do you believe
that women
are not inferior
to men?

do you believe
that men and women
should be paid
the same
for the same work?

congratulations
you're a feminist
it's as simple as that

feminist
is not
a dirty word

<u>life is short</u>

get your education
learn about the world
go and travel
and experience
different cultures

life is short
be reckless
take care of yourself
and go after
what you want

what are you waiting for?

## nice guys

i am so tired
of these so-called
"nice guys"

who pretend
to be allies
of women

but the moment
we refuse
to sleep
with them

they call us bitches
and act
as if
we owe them sex
just because
they aren't dicks to us
(at first)

fuck these "nice guys"
they are wolves
in sheep's clothing

## window shoppers

if he
can't be with you
without looking
at other women
slobbering with desire

he doesn't deserve you

## if you have to ask

if you have to ask
if he loves you
he doesn't

<u>live.</u>

you did what you could
and it didn't last

just accept that

take time
to cry
to mourn
and then
move on

the past is dead
and you are alive
so live.

<u>closure</u>

i'll always wonder
why
things ended
the way they did

and why
i didn't deserve
an explanation

<u>end</u>

when i'm with you
everything else
disappears

when i'm with you
i never want
the moment
to end

and i never want us
to either

<u>with</u>

true love
is just being with someone
not needing
to fill the silence
with unnecessary words

true love
doesn't beg
to be acknowledged

true love
is effortless
and everlasting

## version

there's no version
of myself
i'd rather be
than the one
i am
with you

because you
always bring out
the best
in me

## songs

don't waste
your favorite songs
on lovers
who don't deserve
to be remembered
whenever you hear them

## the truth

the truth is
i will be looking
for pieces of you
in everyone
who comes after you

the truth is
you were everything
i ever wanted
and i'll never
truly
be over you

<u>dreams</u>

i dream
in flashes
of you

our dates
our arguments
our talks

but the problem with dreams
is that they end

just like we did

and with the morning
that fact
slaps me in the face

## looking for love

the worst thing
about love
is that it
cannot
be found
by looking

it has to be
run into
like sleep walking
in the dead of night

it creeps up on you
suddenly
and fiercely

## fall

fall
far and fast
from your perch
of indifference

## obama

barack obama
was a good man
hated for his skin color
and held to a standard
no white man
had ever been held to

and even then
the worst
he did

was wear a tan suit

he rose above
their evil
and is forever
a shining example
of dignity
and a good president

## glass ceiling

i can't help but think
that the world
would be better
if run
by women

its time
for a woman president
to run this country

maybe then
we could have a world
not beholden
to male hormones
and weapons
clearly compensating
for something

<u>war</u>

evil
committed
in the name
of evil
is still
evil

<u>care</u>

show me
you care

touch me
with your love

you are
more than
enough

## broken

even
a broken heart
beats right
twice a day

## sword

forge
your sword

rebel
against patriarchy

take
the high castles

conquer
your destiny

<u>chapter three</u>
send her into battle

.

#

<u>send her into battle</u>

she
can fend
for herself

throw her
into the thick of things

there is nothing
like a woman
backed into a corner

<u>sorry</u>

if he apologizes
but doesn't change
the apology
means nothing

<u>beautiful</u>

every
tiny detail
about you
is beautiful

<u>never</u>

never
throw away
gold
in search
of glitter

<u>burn the fairy tales</u>

throw all of those
ancient, misogynistic
fairy tales
into the fire

let them burn
and let
the tropes
of the damsel
in distress
and exclusively male
heroes
burn too

## loneliness

it's easy
to need
someone
anyone

to fill
your loneliness
when midnight
strikes

but stay strong
it will pass
and you can
get through this

## infinity

don't accept
bad treatment
just because
you always have

stand up
for what
you deserve

and demand
to be treated
the way
you should be

for you
are a goddess
and deserve
no less
than
infinity

## his

you
may
be
his

but
never
forget

you
are
your
own
first
and
foremost

forget

you will never forget
the memories
you made
with him

but fear not

you will, one day
forget
the feelings you had
for him
that now sear their way
into your heart
like a branding iron

fear not
this too shall pass
and you
will
forget

## okay

it's okay
to not
be okay

it's okay
to be

hurting
broken
hopeless
anxious
dying
devastated

just accept
the way you feel
and know this:

the sun will rise
and you
will rise
with it

wolves

beware
most of all
the men
who seek out
vulnerable women

to

control
abuse
hurt
manipulate

they are wolves
preying on the weak
they are evil
incarnate

do not
feed yourself
to the wolves
this
i beg of you

<u>sometimes</u>

sometimes
you've got to walk away
from someone
you love

because you can't love them
without hurting
yourself

## flower

you are not
a flower
sitting pretty
smiling into
a summer breeze

you are
a fucking thunderstorm
raining vengeance
upon the wicked

mirror

i hate the way
i still can't smile
the way
i used to
before
i met you

## masterpiece

you
are an unfinished work

do not compare
your prologue
to someone else's
epilogue

<u>netflix</u>

do not be ashamed
of needing
a day off
to sit
and relax
and put yourself
back together

mental health

if we all
treated mental health
as being
as important
as physical health

our world
would be
a lot
better off

<u>independent</u>

i don't want
to keep putting in hours
for someone else

i want
this book
to sell well
and i want
to live my life
in financial freedom

so please
post about this book
tell your friends
leave reviews

this
is my future
on the line

and it
is in
your hands

solidarity

i think women
need to support other women
a lot more

we turn
altogether too easily
on each other
and see each other
as enemies
when we should
be banding together
in mutual support

## typewriter

there is something
so incredibly
satisfying
about the click
and clack
of a typewriter

moving across
the page
with rigid purpose
and certainty

<u>pets</u>

humanity
does not deserve
the love of animals

we destroy their world
and breed them
to love us

and yet
they do
anyways

if only
we
could be
so good

## honor

if nothing else
i want them
to say
she tried
her best
she did
what she could
she lived
with honor
treating others
with respect
and love

<u>success</u>

success
will never be
a dollar figure
amount

<u>you</u>

hey you
yes you
fucking
fall in love
with me
already

what's holding you back?
=========================

what's holding you back?
is it the past?
is it fear
of failure?

don't worry
you will
rise above
all of that
and you
will get what you want

these things
may hold you back
for now
but don't worry

everything
will be
alright

and your life
will turn out
as wonderful
as your wildest
of dreams

## chapter four
watch her win

#

## watch her win

she
is not afraid
of the storm
because
she is
the storm

so throw challenges
at her

watch her bloom
watch her grow
watch her win

excuses

there will always be
some reason
not to push yourself
to do
the most
you could possibly do

but realize this:
excuses are infinite
but opportunity is not

so choose
opportunity

## giving up

you will take losses
you will lose battles
but that is temporary

giving up
is what makes
it permanent

so don't
ever
give up

## the diamond that crushes

the pursuit
of material gain
above all else
is a trap
waiting
to ensnare you

you will follow
a trail of diamonds
that leads
on and on
and you
will think
you control it

but one day
you will look up
to see one giant diamond
falling

and before you realize it
it's too late

## love yourself

love yourself
the hardest
when it is hardest
to love yourself

## love yourself pt 2

love yourself
for who you are
right now

for all of your flaws
and imperfections
all of your scars
and brokenness

## growing

do not
expect
fruit
from a seed

do not
expect
to have everything
figured out

do not
forget
that you
are still growing
as a person

and its okay
not to have
everything
figured out
just yet

## learn from your mistakes

do not
look down
upon the mistakes
you made
in the past

do not
resent
the person
you used to be

do not
speak badly
of bad choices
you once made

for you
could not be
who you are
today
without having been
who you once were

<u>heartbeat</u>

if your heart
still beats

your story
isn't over

so keep pushing on
the sun will rise
in the morning

## get back up

you may be
knocked down
beaten
broken
winded
and feeling
like you couldn't
possibly
go on

but reach in
for that second wind
of strength
push up
get up from the ground
and face
another day

<u>you</u>

you
were meant
for greatness

you
were meant
to conquer

you
are more
than you seem

you
are a hero
in the making

you
have so much more
to give

and you
can never
be kept down

<u>fear</u>

courage
is doing something
despite fear
not without it

we all
have to get
through it

we all
are capable

fear
will not rule
your life

you
are stronger
than fear

and you
will win
this battle

## look up at the stars

when the night
is silent
and full
of a heavy
darkness

that
is when its most important
to look up
at the stars

## footprints

look back
at the footprints
behind you

you did that
you came this far
and you
will go
so much
further

expect

do not expect
the impossible

do not expect
a rose
to grow
in the dark

and don't search
for love
in people
who could never
love you
the way
you need
to be loved

<u>loss</u>

not everything you lose
is a loss

## misunderstood

she was
the brightest of flame
misunderstood
in the darkness

## potential

never make
the mistake
of falling in love
with someone
for what you see in them
rather than
for who they are

for if you do
you will always
be disappointed

silence

sometimes silence
can leave
the deadliest scars

i asked you
"do you love me?"

and that five seconds
of silence
hurt me more
than your words
ever could have

<u>home</u>

home
can be
a
person

<u>them</u>

how other people
treat you
has nothing
to do
with you

and everything
to do
with them

## too much

you
are not
too much

one day
you will realize
you can only be
too much
to someone
who is
not enough
for you

## change

stop complaining
about your life
and start changing
what you don't like

## there is nothing

there is nothing
more beautiful
or grand

than the sight
of a woman
being
everything
she can be

bloom

never
be ashamed
of what you are
where you've been
or the challenges
you've faced

do not despise
the seed
from which
you bloomed

for that
is what made you
so beautiful

<u>-Adeline Whitmore</u>

if you liked this book
please share it
review it
post about it
and spread the word